A PROUD AND ISOLATED NATION

Americans Take a Stand in Texas 1820-1845

PLEASANT - HILL
APRIL 9ᵗʰ 1864

TITLE LIST

A PROUD AND ISOLATED NATION:

Americans Take a Stand in Texas 1820-1845

BY
SHEILA NELSON

MASON CREST PUBLISHERS
PHILADELPHIA

Mason Crest Publishers Inc.
370 Reed Road
Broomall, Pennsylvania 19008
(866) MCP-BOOK (toll free)

First printing
1 2 3 4 5 6 7 8 9 10

Library of Congress Cataloging-in-Publication Data

Nelson, Sheila.
A proud and isolated nation : Americans take a stand in Texas / by Sheila Nelson.
p. cm. — (How America became America)
Includes bibliographical references (p.) and index.
Audience: Grades 9–12.
ISBN 1-59084-906-X   ISBN 1-59084-900-0 (series)
1. Texas—History—Revolution, 1835–1836—Juvenile literature. 2. Texas—History—Republic, 1836–1846—
Juvenile literature. 3. Texas—History—To 1846—Juvenile literature. I. Title. II. Series.
F390.N46 2005
976.4'03—dc22
2004019465

Design by Dianne Hodack.
Produced by Harding House Publishing Service, Inc.
Cover design by Dianne Hodack.
Printed in the Hashemite Kingdom of Jordan.

CONTENTS

INTRODUCTION

by Dr. Jack Rakove

Today's America is not the same geographical shape as the first American colonies—and the concept of America has evolved as well over the years.

When the thirteen original states declared their independence from Great Britain, most Americans still lived within one or two hours modern driving time from the Atlantic coast. In other words, the Continental Congress that approved the Declaration of Independence on July 4, 1776, was continental in name only. Yet American leaders like George Washington, Benjamin Franklin, and Thomas Jefferson also believed that the new nation did have a continental destiny. They expected it to stretch at least as far west as the Mississippi River, and they imagined that it could extend even further. The framers of the Federal Constitution of 1787 provided that western territories would join the Union on equal terms with the original states. In 1803, President Jefferson brought that continental vision closer to reality by purchasing the vast Louisiana Territory from France. In the 1840s, negotiations with Britain and a war with Mexico brought the United States to the Pacific Ocean.

This expansion created great opportunities, but it also brought serious costs. As Americans surged westward, they created a new economy of family farms and large plantations. But between the Ohio River and the Gulf of Mexico, expansion also brought the continued growth of plantation slavery for millions of African Americans. Political struggle over the extension of slavery west of the Mississippi was one of the major causes of the Civil War that killed hundreds of thousands of Americans in the 1860s but ended with the destruction of slavery. Creating opportunities for American farmers also meant displacing Native Americans from the lands their ancestors had occupied for centuries. The opening of the west encouraged massive immigration not only from Europe but also from Asia, as Chinese workers came to labor in the California Gold Rush and the building of the railroads.

By the end of the nineteenth century, Americans knew that their great age of territorial expansion was over. But immigration and the growth of modern industrial cities continued to change the American landscape. Now Americans moved back and forth across the continent in search of economic opportunities. African Americans left the South in massive numbers and settled in dense concentrations in the cities of the North. The United States remained a magnet for immigration, but new immigrants came increasingly from Mexico, Central America, and Asia.

Ever since the seventeenth century, expansion and migration across this vast landscape have shaped American history. These books are designed to explain how this process has worked. They tell the story of how modern America became the nation it is today.

The landing of Cabeza de Vaca

One
TEXAS: THE PAST

Through the haze of exhaustion, starvation, and raging thirst, Alvar Nuñez Cabeza de Vaca began to notice a noise, gradually growing louder. The roar sounded like waves breaking against the shore. He pulled himself to his knees to look over the edge of the boat. The sky had begun to lighten in the east, streaked with pink. Around him, men lay unconscious, collapsed on top of one another.

The sailing master was the only other conscious man in the boat. Together, he and Cabeza de Vaca rowed the boat along the shore, waiting until dawn to try to bring it to land. When the sun had risen above the horizon, the two men turned the boat to begin looking for a place to land.

Suddenly, a huge wave lifted the little craft, flinging it toward the shore. For a moment, the boat seemed to hang on the wave, but then the force of the water drove it onto the shore. Men tumbled out into the shallow water, waking with the shock of the landing.

The men crawled onto the beach, dragging themselves on their hands and knees. On the sand, the Spaniards pulled themselves to their feet and gathered driftwood to build a fire. Some found puddles of rainwater they could drink, while others roasted their last handfuls of dried corn over the fire. The men started to feel better as the water slid down their parched throats and the fire began to warm their chilled bodies.

They had set out in the open boat from the coast of Florida over a month before, and it was now early November 1528. Four other boats, the remains of a party of Spanish explorers led by Panfilo de Narvaez, had left Florida at the same

same time, nearly two hundred and fifty men in all. Only two boats survived the voyage, the other coming to shore several miles further along the coast.

Cabeza de Vaca and his men had landed very close to what is now Galveston, Texas. They were not the first Europeans to set foot in Texas, however; another party of Spanish explorers had mapped the coastline nine years before. For the next four years, Cabeza de Vaca and his companions lived with several different groups of Indians. Some of the Indians treated them well, while others enslaved and abused them.

Cabeza de Vaca performed surgery on a Native he encountered on his travels.

By 1532, only four men remained of the eighty who had washed ashore in Texas. The others had gradually been killed by disease, starvation, cold, or by the Indians.

In 1532, the four remaining men set out inland to try and make their way to the Spanish colonies in Mexico. Finally, after traveling across country for several years, in 1536 the men arrived on the west coast of Mexico and came upon a Spanish ship, which took them back to Spain.

After Cabeza de Vaca returned home to Spain, he wrote an account of his experiences in Texas. In his book, he described riches of gold, lead, iron, and copper. He was vague, however, on the exact location of the wealth, and he also wrote that Texas was a "worthless land best left alone." His descriptions of wealth did inspire another Spanish expedition, this one led by Francisco Vazquez de Coronado, but Vazquez de Coronado never found the treasure Cabeza de Vaca wrote about. For the next century and a half, Spain mostly ignored Texas. Occasional Spanish explorers traveled through parts of Texas, but Spain's attention focused on Florida more closely, where the English presence had moved dangerously close to the Spanish colonies.

Cabaza de Vaca and the coast of Texas where he landed

11

The First Texans

For thousands of years, Native American tribes had had Texas all to themselves. Several large tribes lived in the area—tribes such as the Caddo, the Karankawa, the Coathuiltecan, the Lipan, the Apache, the Tonkawa, and the Comanche—themselves divided up into smaller bands. Although the tribes were all Native Americans, their cultures were quite distinct from each other.

The Caddo Indians, for example, lived in eastern and northeastern Texas in established farming communities. One group of Caddos, the Hasinai Caddos, gave Texas its name in 1689, when they encountered a group of Spanish explorers. The Hasinai, who had met Spaniards before, greeted the Europeans, calling out "Taychas!" which they understood to mean "friend" in Spanish. The Spanish thought the Hasinai were giving their tribal name and began calling them the Tejas. Later, the word came to refer to the entire region of eastern Texas and eventually, to the state.

In 1682, Spain became suddenly interested in occupying Texas again, when the French explorer René-Robert Cavelier de La Salle traveled down from Canada to the mouth of the Mississippi, claiming the Mississippi Valley and the area around it in the name of France and calling it Louisiana. Relations between France and Spain had often been uneasy, sometimes erupting into long and violent wars. Now, after he had claimed Louisiana, La Salle traveled to France to argue that forts should be built around the mouth of the Mississippi River and throughout Louisiana in preparation for an attack on Spanish Texas and Mexico.

La Salle returned from France with men and ships to begin building his forts, but quickly ran into problems. Of the three ships that left France, pirates captured one in the West Indies, one sank when trying to sail through a narrow inlet, and the last ran aground on a sandbar.

Comanche

Caddo

Apache

Tonkawa

Lipan

Karankawas

Coahuil-
tecan

Texas Natives

13

More Native Texans

Comanchi village

The Karankawa Indians lived along the Gulf Coast, near where Galveston and Corpus Christi are today. They lived on fish and shellfish, as well as animals they could hunt on land, and nuts and berries they could find. The Karankawas moved around constantly, never staying in one camp for more than a few weeks. When Cabeza de Vaca and his men washed ashore in Texas, a group of Karankawas rescued them and for a time welcomed them into their tribe.

Southern Texas and northeastern Mexico was Coahuiltecan land, where hundreds of similar groups of Indians lived. These Indians migrated around their region, hunting and gathering. After Cabeza de Vaca and his three companions left the Karankawas to look for a Spanish outpost, they encountered the Coahuiltecan and lived with them for a while.

The Lipan were a subgroup of the Apache tribe who moved south through the center of Texas during the sixteenth and seventeenth centuries. After the Europeans brought horses, the Lipan became skilled riders, and their enemies respected their skill as warriors. They were expert hunters, and in later years, they sometimes helped the settlers fight against other Indian tribes. In the Texas War of Independence against Mexico, the Lipan fought on the side of the Texans. Other groups of Apache Indians moved away from the Lipan into western Texas.

The Comanche migrated south from Wyoming in the seventeenth and eighteenth centuries, moving toward Texas and pushing tribes like the Apaches south ahead of them.

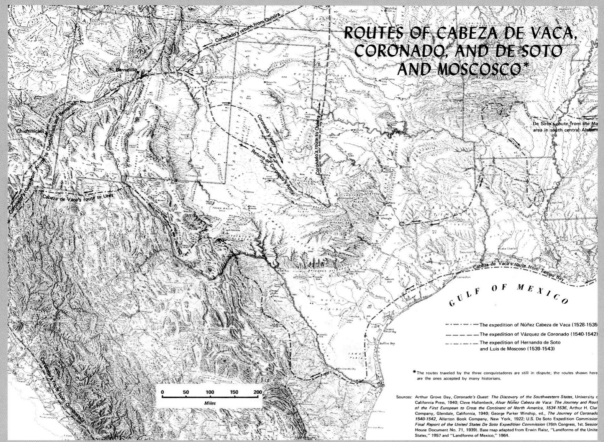

Map of Spanish explorers' routes

Worse, lacking maps of the area and accurate navigational equipment, La Salle completely missed the mouth of the Mississippi he had aimed for and ended up nearly five hundred miles away in Matagorda Bay, in Texas. For months, La Salle tried to find his way back to the Mississippi, making short trips out from Fort St. Louis, which he had built near Matagorda Bay. Finally, in 1686, he set out inland, again heading for the Mississippi, but was murdered by his

15

People of the Wolf

A Lipan warrior

Much of central Texas was occupied by the Tonkawa Indians, centered around the area where Austin is located today. The name Tonkawa means "people of the wolf," because the Tonkawas believed they had descended from a wolf. For this reason, they refused to kill wolves. They also preferred to hunt rather than farm, because hunting was more wolf-like and farming was too tame.

own men near what is now Navasota, Texas.

When the Spanish learned of La Salle's presence in Texas and the plans France had made for their Louisiana territory, they hurriedly began fortifying eastern Texas to protect against the spread of France and other foreign nations. From the Rio Grande up through east Texas, they built a series of missions—"el camino real," or "the king's highway." Over thirty of these missions were constructed, including the Concepcion Mission and the Alamo. Each mission included a complete village, with a wall surrounding a central plaza.

Every time the Spanish started to worry about other countries trying to move into their New World colonies, Texas became important to them. When times were peaceful and foreign nations did not seem to pose a threat, Spain more or less ignored Texas.

In the early 1820s, American settlers began

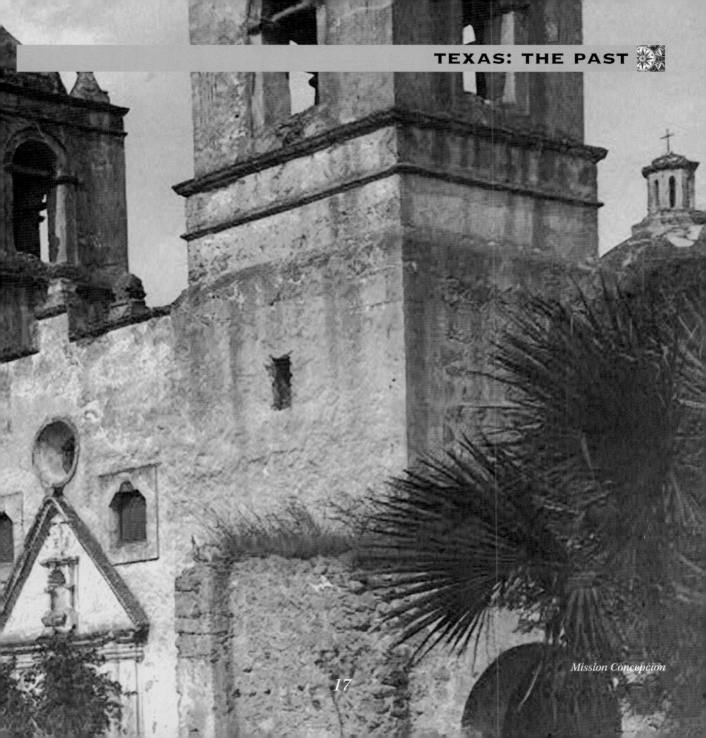

Mission Concepcion

*An **entrepreneur** is someone who assumes the risks of running a business.*

Moses Austin

moving into Texas, despite the Spanish desire to keep them out. Moses Austin, an American ***entrepreneur*** who had founded the American lead industry, tried to gain permission from the Spanish governor of Texas, Antonio María Martínez, to settle in Texas. In 1798, Moses had moved to Louisiana—then in the hands of the Spanish—renounced his American citizenship, and built a town around a lead mine in present-day Potosi, Missouri. In 1819, he started thinking about moving south again, across the border into Texas. He wanted to establish a settlement of hardworking American pioneers in Texas. He had seen how American settlers hungered for space to spread out and thought he could probably make a good profit selling land.

The Spanish did not want American settlers crossing their borders into Texas. They had seen how the United States had already spread. Settlers had moved further and further west; by 1820, the United States even owned Louisiana, which bordered on Spanish territory. Governor Martínez had been ordered by his superiors not to help any Americans who crossed into Texas. Therefore, when Moses Austin came looking for permission to build a settlement, the governor refused his request and ordered him to leave San Antonio immediately. Before Moses departed, however, he ran into an old friend, the Baron de Bastrop, whom he had known in Louisiana. Bastrop invited Moses to stay with him for Christmas, and Moses had a chance to share his ideas with his host. When Bastrop heard Moses' plan, and his argument that he would be able to help Spain keep control over the American settlers, he accompanied Moses back to Governor Martínez the day after

Battle flag, pre-restoration view

19

Ulterior Motives

Difficulties governing the local Indian tribes convinced first the Spanish and then the Mexican governments to allow Americans to settle in Texas. Spain had had difficulty recruiting Spanish settlers to colonize Texas. They hoped bringing in American settlers would help get the land away from the Indians and that the Americans would be easier to control than the Indians.

Requirements for Americans Settling in Texas

Before the Spanish would allow American immigrants to move into Texas, Moses Austin had to agree to three requirements on behalf of the settlers. Each settler would:

1. Be a member of or convert to the Roman Catholic Church.
2. Become a citizen of Texas, swearing allegiance to Spain.
3. Provide a letter of recommendation giving a character reference.

Texas settlers

21

Christmas. With his friend Bastrop's support, this time Moses received the governor's permission to establish a settlement.

As soon as he got back to the United States, Moses Austin began recruiting people to buy land in his new community. Unfortunately, Moses had developed pneumonia on his trip home from Texas. Too excited about the "Texas Venture" to care about his health, Moses threw all his energy into signing up settlers. At the same time, he prepared to leave for Texas himself. Before he could set out for his new colony, however, he came down with a fever. When he realized he was dying, he begged his wife to write to their son Stephen and to "tell dear Stephen that it is his dieing father's last request to prosecute [carry on] the enterprise he had commenced."

His son complied with his father's deathbed request. One of the first problems Stephen Austin faced, however, was convincing the Mexican government to honor the land grant issued to his father. On September 27, 1821, Mexico had finally succeeded in winning its independence from Spain. When Stephen arrived in December with the first settlers, the new Mexican government claimed Moses Austin's grant had come from the Spanish government and was therefore invalid.

Quickly, Stephen hurried to Mexico City to argue on behalf of the American settlement. Finally, on January 3, 1823, Stephen succeeded in convincing the Mexican emperor to sign a law giving Stephen the right to settle three hundred families in Texas. The head of each family would receive "a league and a labor" of land—4,605 acres (almost 19 square km). These first three hundred families became known as "the Old Three Hundred." Most of them were of Scots-Irish background, coming from the southern United States. Over the next fifteen years, tens of thousands more American settlers would arrive in Texas.

Americans had now established a presence in Texas, mostly in the eastern part of the territory. They had come despite the fact that neither Spain nor Mexico had really wanted them there. The miles of wild Texas countryside drew them on as they dreamed of farms and lands they could make their own.

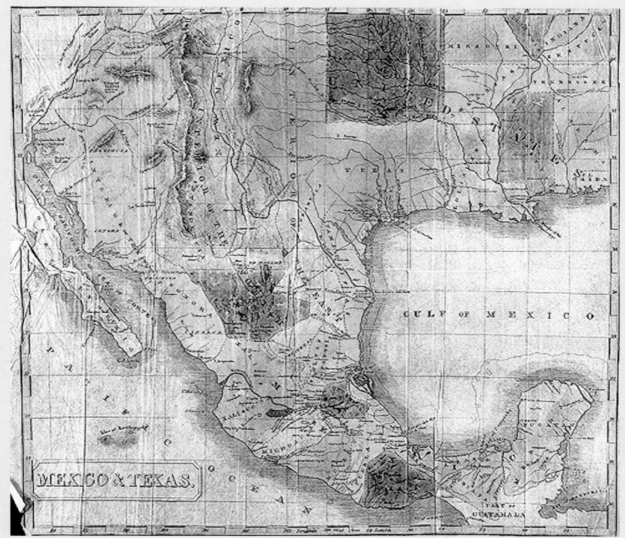

Map of Mexico and Texas

The Capitol in 1829

Two
THE UNITED STATES IN THE 1830s

The Capitol building overflowed with people on Wednesday, March 4, 1829. Thousands had traveled from across the United States to witness the *inauguration* of President Andrew Jackson. In his election campaign, Jackson had championed the common people. The people loved him for his ordinary roots. He had grown up in the backwoods of South Carolina, and later had become a military hero fighting in the Creek War (an Indian *civil war*) and the War of 1812. As a military general, Jackson had earned the nickname "Old Hickory," because his men said he was as tough as hickory wood. The soldiers who served under him said Old Hickory was a good commander—but not a man to be crossed.

While campaigning for the election of 1828, Jackson often pointed out that he had been robbed of the election in 1824, and that he had been the true choice of the people for President. In 1824, Jackson had received the most popular votes, as well as the most electoral votes. Since the vote had been split between four candidates, though, he had not received the majority of electoral votes. Therefore, the outcome of the election had to be decided by Congress. Jackson had been furious when Congress elected John Quincy Adams as President. He gathered

An *inauguration* is a ceremony swearing someone into office.

A *civil war* is a military conflict between opposing groups within a country.

The Electoral College

One of the problems facing the Constitutional Convention was the decision on the best way to elect the president. One alternative was to have Congress choose the president. This was rejected because of the concern that it could lead to corruption or upset the balance of power. Another method considered was for the state legislature to elect the president. Many felt that this would lead to the erosion of federal authority. The last option was election through direct popular vote. The Constitutional Convention rejected direct vote because of the concern that, due to the difficulty in getting information out, people would vote only for their "favorite sons."

The Electoral College was a compromise. It would allow voters to vote for electors who would then cast their votes for the candidates. The total number of a state's electors is equal to the number of senators, two, and the number of representatives, which is based on the state's population. On the Monday following the second Wednesday in December, the electors meet in their respective state capitals to cast their ballots for president and vice president. The backs are sealed, and delivered to the president of the Senate. On January 6, in front of both houses of Congress, the ballots are opened and read.

Most of the time the electors cast their ballots for the candidate who received the most popular vote. There have been exceptions. Four presidents have been elected although they did not receive the most popular vote: John Quincy Adams, Rutherford B. Hayes, Benjamin Hayes, and George W. Bush.

Aristocrats are members of the highest social class in a country.

the support of the American people over the next four years, representing himself as the people's candidate.

When Jackson won the 1828 election, many Americans felt they had won a victory for the common man over the *aristocrats*. Over fifteen thousand people attended Jackson's inauguration. Jackson's

Andrew Jackson's inauguration

The American Dream

Americans believed they could accomplish anything they dreamed about. The United States was the land of opportunity, where anyone, no matter his background, could strike it rich or rise through the political ranks, maybe even becoming President. With hard work, anything was possible.

opponent, John Quincy Adams, did not.

After the ceremony, many people followed Jackson back to the White House for a celebration party. The presidential mansion filled up quickly. The politicians and wealthy families from the area came to the party, as did hundreds of ordinary people who were proud to have elected a man they considered one of themselves.

The celebration soon became rowdy. People broke dishes and dropped glasses. Some climbed on top of furniture to catch sight of the President, leaving muddy footprints on the upholstery. Finally, Jackson slipped out a back

Andrew Jackson and writing from his inaugural address

door to get away. He spent his first night as President sleeping at a nearby hotel. Eventually, the White House staff carried casks of wine and tubs of ice cream out onto the front lawn to coax people outside.

Some of Jackson's political opponents considered the party an appalling disgrace, but most Jacksonian Democrats thought it represented a triumph of the common man. The President's inauguration had become a celebration for the entire country, not just the wealthy or those in high society.

As the United States developed as a country, the people began to develop a distinctly

29

*Someone who has a strong **work ethic** is dedicated to work or to the belief in the moral value of hard work.*

***Apprenticing** means working with someone skilled in a profession for a period of time to learn the job.*

*A **tariff** is duty or tax placed by the government on certain, usually imported, goods.*

*If something is **imported**, it is brought from another country.*

*An **agrarian** society is one based on farming.*

American self-concept. They were proud of their country, with its ideals of democracy and freedom. More and more, the United States grew away from its European roots. Americans valued things like egalitarianism—equality among people without regard to social class—and a strong **work ethic**. Americans saw themselves as standing strong and alone, dependent on no other nation. Like a young adult who no longer needs her parents' support, the United States had left her "mother country"—England—far behind, and Americans took great pride in being different—and better—than the European nations.

When Andrew Jackson won the presidential election, everything the American people believed to be true about the United States was confirmed. Jackson had been left an orphan at age fourteen and had prospered by **apprenticing** himself to a saddle maker, studying law, and then serving as a major general in the army. He was the first President who did not come from an aristocratic background. Jackson was a military hero, tough but well-respected. He claimed to be a representative of the common people and many Americans saw him as a symbol of the American Dream.

One of the greatest conflicts the United States faced in the 1830s involved the debate over slavery. By this time, slavery had been outlawed in all of the northern states and the country had begun to divide into free states and slave states, a line drawn between those who owned slaves and those who believed slavery was evil.

In 1828, the year before Jackson had become President, Congress had enacted an extremely high **tariff**, designed to protect

A

PICTURE OF SLAVERY,

FOR YOUTH.

BY

THE AUTHOR OF "THE BRANDED HAND" AND "CHATTELIZED HUMANITY."

Philanthropy imploring America to release the Slave and revive Liberty.

Undo the heavy burthen, let the oppressed go free, break every yoke.

BOSTON:

PUBLISHED BY J. WALKER AND W. R. BLISS,

AND FOR SALE AT THE ANTI-SLAVERY OFFICE, 21 CORNHILL; BELA MARSH, 25 CORNHILL; ALSO AT THE ANTI-SLAVERY OFFICES IN NEW YORK, 142 NASSAU ST.; AND IN PHILADELPHIA, 31 NORTH FIFTH ST.

Antislavery pamphlet

Andrew Jackson's inauguration

the sales of northern manufactured goods by taxing **imported** foreign goods. Unfortunately, the **agrarian** South was dependent on imported goods since it did not manufacture goods itself. The tariff hurt Southerners nearly as much as it protected the northern states. Also, Britain, the largest purchaser of southern cotton, started threatening to look for other suppliers, since it had become so expensive to buy from the United States.

In 1832, Jackson modified the tariff slightly, lowering the tax only a little. Southern states were not satisfied by the changes. The tariff reforms had not

been great enough to improve their problems. South Carolina especially protested the high tariffs.

On November 4, 1832, South Carolina passed the Ordinance of Nullification, declaring that the tariffs of 1828 and 1832 were **null and void** within the borders of South Carolina, since Congress had exceeded its **constitutional authority** when it had passed the tariffs. By making this declaration, South Carolina asserted the right of individual states to question the authority of the federal government. Similarly, Kentucky and Virginia had declared the Alien and Sedition Acts void in 1798.

President Jackson firmly believed that the federal government was the ultimate law of the United States. He thought individual states had rights, but they could not conflict with whatever the federal government decided. He believed the South Carolina Ordinance of Nullification was a threat to national unity. Quickly, he issued a proclamation to South Carolina, declaring that they had no right not to obey federal law; their ordinance was **treasonous**, Jackson said. To back up his proclamation, Jackson sent U.S. Navy ships to the Charleston harbor to make sure the tariffs were paid.

Finally, Senator Henry Clay of Kentucky introduced a tariff bill in Congress that would gradually bring the taxes down over the next ten years. After the bill passed, South Carolina backed down and repealed their Ordinance of Nullification. Both President Jackson and South Carolina thought they had won a victory in the dispute. South Carolina had repealed the ordinance—as Jackson wanted—but only after they had gotten more or less what they wanted.

*Something that is **null and void** is valueless and has no legal standing.*

*Powers granted to the U.S. government by the U.S. Constitution are its **constitutional authority**.*

***Treasonous** means relating to the betrayal of a country.*

African American slaves

*To **secede** means to break away formally from a group or alliance.*

The Nullification Crisis had important implications for slavery. The southern states worried the federal government would soon try to outlaw slavery completely. If the Ordinance of Nullification had been completely successful, they could have used the same method to deal with a ban on slavery. Since it had not succeeded as South Carolina had hoped, however, the South would have to try a different response to laws against slavery. Thirty years later, when southern states feared the election of Abraham Lincoln would mean just such a ban, they would choose to **secede** from the United States altogether, rather than try to work within the existing government.

Jackson himself owned more than a hundred slaves who worked on the large plantation, the Hermitage, he had built in Tennessee. His party, the Democrats, supported slavery, and most Democratic politicians were also slave owners. Jackson was said to be kind but strict with his slaves, treating them in much the same way as he treated his men when he served as a military general.

Despite Jackson's reputation among his supporters of the time as a champion of ordinary people, he often tried hard to benefit the large aristocratic plantation owners of the South, and clearly he did not consider black people and Indians to be the equals of white Americans. In this, he was much like most other Americans of his time. On an individual level, he could be very kind to blacks and Indians. For example, while he was fighting against the Creek Indians, he found a ten-month-old baby Indian boy whose parents had died in the battle. He rescued the baby, and, when he could not find anyone to take him in, carried him home to his wife and raised

Jackson's plantation, the Hermitage

Henry Clay

Signing of the Treaty of Fort Jackson

the boy as his son. Jackson's policies toward the Indians as a group, however, were often extremely harsh. In 1814, having defeated the Creek Indians, Jackson got the Creeks to sign the Treaty of Fort Jackson, which gave 23 million acres of their land to the United States.

In 1830, President Jackson signed the Indian Removal Act, which would take tribes of eastern Indians, living in settled states, and resettle them in specially designated districts west of the Mississippi River in Indian Territory (now the state of Oklahoma). In the early 1800s, Thomas Jefferson had begun moving Indian tribes west of the Mississippi to make room for white settlers in the eastern United States. Jefferson had made it clear that those tribes who "became civilized" could stay on their eastern land. Tribes like the Cherokee, Chickasaw, Choctaw, Creek, and Seminole had done their best to become part of the civilization of the white settlers. Many had intermarried with Europeans and lived settled lives in farming communities. The Cherokee had written their own constitution, based on the United States Constitution, had started a newspaper, and had built roads, schools, and churches.

As immigrants poured into the United States, however, land became scarce. The Indians had land; the settlers wanted it. Suddenly, it was not enough that some of the native tribes had become very much like white Americans.

At first, the Cherokee in Georgia tried to fight the Indian Removal Act by taking the government to court. In 1832, the Supreme Court ruled that the act was unconstitutional. Despite the Court's ruling, Indian removal continued. President Jackson ignored the Supreme Court's verdict, handed down by Chief Justice John Marshall. The President is reported to have said, "John Marshall has made his decision. Now let him enforce it!" By the end of the decade, tens of thousands of Indians had been moved west. Thousands died on the long, difficult march, which became known as the Trail of Tears.

The Trail of Tears

The Trail of Tears

The United States of the 1830s was not kind to Indians. As the country's population grew, and along with it the demand for land, Indians were the first to pay the price. As a result, the government enacted a policy of forced removal. The most famous was the Trail of Tears, the journey of the Cherokee Indians from northern Georgia to "Indian Territory" (present-day Oklahoma).

At first, Georgia passed a series of anti-Cherokee laws. Property was confiscated, Cherokee were not allowed to testify in court, and it was illegal for Cherokee to speak out against westward immigration. A lottery was held to distribute the Cherokee land to whites.

Despite a Supreme Court ruling, numerous attempts at negotiations, and ignored treaties, President Martin Van Buren ordered the removal of the Cherokee in May 1838. Over a three-week period, General Winfield Scott and seven thousand soldiers rounded up between 17,000 and 18,000 Cherokee from northern Georgia, Arkansas, Tennessee, and Alabama (along with approximately two thousand slaves). They were removed and with only the clothes on their backs, they were sent to Rattlesnake Springs and Ross's Landing, both in Tennessee, where they began the walk to Indian Territory. The Indians were divided into twenty groups for the trip. Between four thousand and eight thousand Cherokee died on the approximately 1,200-mile walk.

A Creek house

Andrew and Rachel

Andrew Jackson loved his wife Rachel fiercely. When she was seventeen years old, Rachel Donelson had married Lewis Robards. Robards turned out to be unreasonably jealous, accusing Rachel of unfaithfulness with several men and making her life miserable. In 1790, the Kentucky legislature told Robards he could divorce his wife, since he believed she had been unfaithful to him. Rachel moved out, believing she was now divorced. In 1791, she married Andrew Jackson.

In 1793, Robards finally got around to divorcing Rachel, using the fact that she was living with Jackson as grounds for the divorce. Andrew and Rachel were horrified; their marriage had not been legal, since Rachel had not been divorced after all. In 1794, they married again to make it official.

The scandal of his marriage and "adultery" continued to haunt Jackson in his political career. He was intensely protective of Rachel, allowing no one to insult her. This, combined with Jackson's fiery temper, led to a number of duels in her honor.

In 1806, Charles Dickinson made a comment about Rachel, and Jackson called him out for a duel. Jackson determined to kill Dickinson, even "if he had shot me through the brain." Dickinson shot first, hitting Jackson in the chest. Ignoring the pain (those with him did not even realize he had been shot until later), Jackson coolly aimed his pistol at Dickinson and fired, killing him. Dickinson's bullet remained lodged in Jackson's chest, causing him pain for the rest of his life.

Rachel died only months after Jackson had been elected President in 1828, before his inauguration. Bitterly, Jackson blamed her death on those who had harassed her throughout the campaign by slandering her character.

Andrew Jackson

The Trail of Tears

The Indian Removal Act of 1830

The Indian Removal Act allowed for the creation of districts west of the Mississippi River, onto which eastern Indian tribes would be moved. Some tribes moved west willingly, but others, such as the Cherokee, were forcibly marched west on the Trail of Tears.

An Act to provide for an exchange of lands with the Indians residing in any of the states or territories, and for their removal west of the river Mississippi:

Be it enacted by the Senate and House of Representatives of the United States of America, in Congress assembled, That it shall and may be lawful for the President of the United States to cause so much of any territory belonging to the United States, west of the river Mississippi, not included in any state or organized territory, and to which the Indian title has been extinguished, as he may judge necessary, to be divided into a suitable number of districts, for the reception of such tribes or nations of Indians as may choose to exchange the lands where they now reside, and remove there; and to cause each of said districts to be so described by natural or artificial marks, as to be easily distinguished from every other. . . .

And be it further enacted, That upon the making of any such exchange [of eastern lands for western ones] as is contemplated by this act, it shall and may be lawful for the President to cause such aid and assistance to be furnished to the emigrants as may be necessary and proper to enable them to remove to, and settle in, the country for which they may have exchanged; and also, to give them such aid and assistance as may be necessary for their support and subsistence for the first year after their removal.

The cabin where Davy Crockett was born

Three
TEXAS UNDER MEXICAN RULE

According to the story, when Davy Crockett was on his way to Washington to start serving as a United States Congressman from Tennessee, he met a man at an inn who shouted "Hurray for Adams!" Davy was a Jackson man; he did not think much of President Adams, and he told the man so. "Who are you, anyway?" the man demanded.

Davy answered, "I am that same David Crockett, fresh from the backwoods, half horse, half alligator, a little touched with the snapping-turtle. I can wade the Mississippi, leap the Ohio, ride upon a streak of lightning, and slip without a scratch down a honey-locust. I can whip my weight in wildcats, and, if any gentleman pleases, for a ten-dollar bill he can throw in a panther. I can hug a bear too close for comfort, and eat any man opposed to General Jackson."

Whether or not Davy Crockett actually said this is hard to say. Fact and fiction are so closely entwined that separating them is almost impossible, especially when in the midst of the tangle stood Davy Crockett, wearing a coonskin cap and buckskin clothes, wrestling bears and twisting the tail off Haley's Comet. The public loved this Davy, and the tall tales published about him grew wilder and more outrageous.

David Crockett, the backwoods politician from Tennessee, was far more than a tall tale, however. Crockett had come to Washington in 1827 as a Democrat, believing strongly in the ideals represented by Andrew Jackson. He had fought under Jackson in the Creek War and respected him. He supported Jackson in his cam-

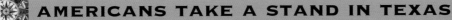

Squatters are people who live on a piece of land illegally.

Davy Crockett

paign for President, celebrating the victory of the common man along with the rest of America when Jackson won the election.

After Jackson became President, however, Crockett began having some disagreements with him. One of the first problems concerned Crockett's Land Bill. Crockett had introduced the Land Bill in Congress, which would give poor *squatters* in Tennessee the right to cheaply buy the land they lived on. The Land Bill was one of the main reasons

The Davy Crockett almanac

Crockett had wanted to become a congressman. When Jackson failed to support the bill, Crockett was furious. Crockett's support of Jackson ended altogether after Jackson passed the Indian Removal Act in 1830. Crockett firmly opposed the bill and refused to compromise his belief that it was wrong by voting for it, even though his colleagues told him he should support it to keep the President happy.

After this, Crockett lost the next election in 1831 and went back

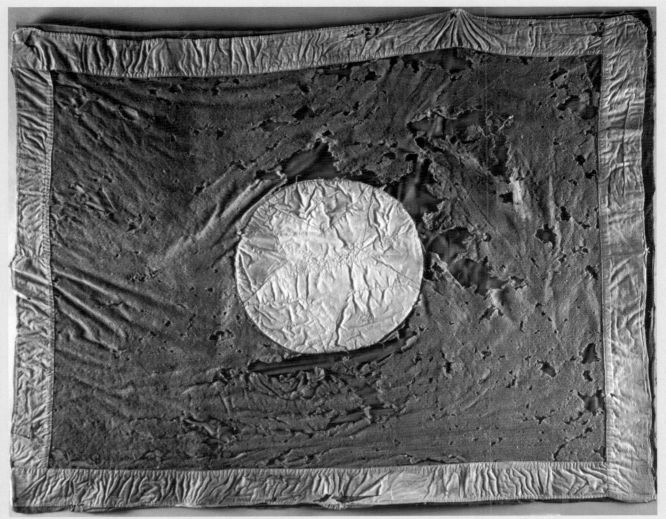

Granbury's brigade flag, Texas 6th infantry and 15th calvary

*A **racist** is someone who believes people of one race are superior to those of other races.*

to Tennessee. He returned to Congress in 1833, this time as a Whig. He spent most of his time criticizing President Jackson. Davy Crockett's popular image had taken hold by this time. People loved the Davy Crockett Almanac, filled with incredible stories of Davy's life in the wilderness. Each edition contained wilder stories, until, ten years after the real Crockett's death. The stories told about Davy roaming the country with his pet bear "Death Hug" and having adventures like riding an alligator up Niagara Falls.

At first, Crockett did not mind his increasing popularity, and even played it up sometimes. He occasionally wore coonskin caps, instead of his usual hat. Once, Crockett went to the theater to see the play *The Lion of the West,* a play supposedly about a character named Nimrod Wildfire, although everyone knew the play was really about Davy Crockett. Before the performance, the actor playing Wildfire acknowledged Crockett's presence with a bow. When Crockett stood and bowed back, the audience went wild.

As the stories got crazier, though, Crockett sometimes wanted to leave his image behind. He had not succeeded as a politician. The Tennessee Land Bill had never passed, and he had failed in blocking the Indian Removal Act. Now, the stories all portrayed him as larger than life, a close friend of President Jackson, and a **racist** Indian killer—things with which he did not want to be associated.

In 1835, Crockett lost the congressional election. His opponent had used the Davy of the stories against Crockett, accusing him of drinking and womanizing. He had also brought up the fact that Crockett had accomplished very little as a congressman. The peo-

Sam Houston

The Alamo as it looked in the 1830s

ple loved Davy Crockett, but they wanted him as their folk hero, fighting bears in the Tennessee wilderness, not wearing a suit as a Washington politician.

After losing the election, Crockett was quoted as saying, "You may all go to hell and I will go to Texas!" Over the last few years,

Crockett had been thinking a lot about Texas. Sam Houston, once governor of Tennessee, had told him about Texas several years earlier and Crockett had been fascinated.

At first, Crockett just meant to travel around Texas, exploring it thoroughly and doing some hunting. When he arrived, however, he changed his mind. He met Texans who were trying to win their independence from Mexico, and he decided to join them. He signed an oath of allegiance to the new independent Texas government and traveled south to the Alamo, an old mission-turned-fort near the city of San Antonio de Bexar, where a group of settlers had

51

Repeal *means to officially revoke or abolish a law.*

decided to take a stand against the Mexicans. Crockett had become very tired of Washington politics and the air of Texas reenergized him. Suddenly, he was overflowing with excitement and ideas; he planned to take up politics again in Texas and work as a land agent.

Meanwhile, Texas had been trying for years to convince Mexico to grant them independence. At the same time, the Mexican government tried unsuccessfully to stop the flow of American settlers crossing its borders. In 1830, Mexico, fearing Texas could soon fall into the hands of the United States since so many of its residents were American, passed a law prohibiting further settlement. Stephen Austin, the government administrator overseeing the American settlements, discovered a loophole in the law, however, which let him keep bringing in new colonists.

Angry with their treatment at the hand of the Mexican government, Texans petitioned the government to let them form their own state, since they were still a part of the southern Mexican state Coahuila. If they governed their own state, they thought, they would at least have a little more control over their own affairs. Mexican President Antonio López de Santa Anna later agreed to **repeal** the law forbidding immigration, but he refused to grant the Texans' request for statehood.

The first armed conflict between American settlers and Mexican troops occurred in 1832. Colonel Juan Bradburn, who commanded the fort at Anahuac on the Gulf of Mexico, arrested nearly twenty prominent Americans living in the area and had

Battle at Fort Anahuac

Stephen Austin

them held at the fort awaiting transportation for military trial. Bradburn refused to give a reason for the arrests. The settlers at Brazoria, down the coast, loaded a cannon onto a schooner and headed down the Brazos River, intending to sail up the coast to Anahuac and attack the fort. At the mouth of the river sat Fort Velasco, under the command of Colonel Domingo Ugartechea. He refused to let the schooner pass, since he knew where the settlers were headed and why.

On June 26, the Americans attacked Fort Velasco, surrounding it and firing on the soldiers standing on the walkways just below the tops of the walls. Beginning at midnight, the battle raged for nine hours. By nine in the morning, almost three-quarters of the Mexicans had been killed or wounded, and Colonel Ugartechea agreed to surrender, on the condi-

tion that his men would be treated honorably and allowed to take a ship back to Mexico. The Americans accepted the conditions and the surrender, winning the opening battle in the Texas Revolution.

A few weeks after the Battle of Velasco, Mexican forces arrived with five warships and four hundred men to subdue the rebellion. The Americans claimed they had only acted in support of General Santa Anna, who was then running for election against President Bustamente. (Colonel Bradburn, of Fort Anahuac, had been strongly in support of Bustamente and against Santa Anna.) The Mexicans were suspicious, but they let the matter go.

Antonio López de Santa Anna was a Mexican hero in 1832. Ever since Mexico had won its independence from Spain in 1821, the country had been chaotic and unstable. As the highest

American ship on its way to Fort Velasco

Santa Anna

ranking general in the country, Santa Anna had become wildly popular after he had led Mexican troops to defeat the Spanish when they invaded in 1829. After this, he began calling himself the Savior of the Fatherland.

In 1833, Santa Anna became President of Mexico. He was not really interested in the actual running of the country, however; he just wanted the prestige that went along with his position. He quickly turned the actual administrative duties over to his vice president. After a year, he decided the Mexican people were not yet ready to handle democracy. He fired his vice president and declared himself a dictator.

As dictator, Santa Anna made sweeping changes in the Mexican government. He disbanded Congress and dissolved the constitution. Although some of the wealthy, conservative Mexicans approved of his actions, many, including the American settlers in Texas, were appalled.

Santa Anna's extreme actions only provoked the Texans, who already chafed under Mexican rule. Soon, the unrest would erupt into open rebellion. The Americans who had settled in Texas carried with them the same independent spirit, belief in democracy and freedom, and trust that hard work could get a man anywhere that characterized Americans all over the United States. They could not bear to be under the control of a dictator for long.

The Texas where Davy Crockett would arrive in 1836 was a battlefield. And Davy had never run from a fight.

Santa Anna and his officers

"Battalion Guerrero Battle Flag," pre-restoration view

Four

TEXAS FIGHTS FOR INDEPENDENCE

The small American settlement of Gonzales owned one small cannon, given to them by the Mexican government in 1831 to help defend against Indian attacks. The cannon was nearly useless, having been altered to make it harder to fire. Nevertheless, it was better than nothing.

As dictator, Santa Anna began a process of disarmament throughout the settlements of Texas. Anyone who tried to resist him, he attacked and destroyed. And in 1835, a letter arrived in Gonzales, demanding the return of the cannon. The settlers sent back a letter stating that they still needed the cannon for defense, and asked to be excused from having to give it up. In response, Lieutenant Francisco Castaneda and more than a hundred men headed for Gonzales with orders to retrieve the cannon. As they got closer, the Mexicans started hearing rumors about men massing in the town.

The American settlers had finally had enough. They took their cannon, buried it in a peach orchard, and prepared to defend their town. Men arrived from neighboring settlements to help.

On September 29, 1835, Castaneda and his men arrived at the Guadalupe River. Gonzales was just a couple of miles away, on the other side of the river. Usually, people could easily cross the river by fording it or taking a boat or raft. Now, though, the river was flooding, and the settlers had taken all the boats and rafts to the other side of the river.

COME AND TAKE IT

Flag from the Battle of Gonzales

Castaneda shouted across the rushing water to the men on the far bank. The Americans informed him that the person he needed to talk to about the cannon was Andrew Ponton, who was out of town. Castaneda would have to wait.

For several days the Mexicans waited, while more men arrived on the other side of the river to defend Gonzales. In only a few days, the number of fighting men in the tiny town swelled from eighteen to close to two hundred.

The Americans speculated on what the Mexicans would do. They decided Castaneda would wait until reinforcements arrived from San Antonio de Bexar and then cross the river to attack them. (In reality, Castaneda had orders to avoid a battle and was waiting not for reinforcements but for further orders.)

The Americans decided they needed to attack first. They dug up the cannon, repaired it, and gathered scrap metal to use as shot. On the night of October 1, under cover of darkness, they crossed the river several miles downstream of the Mexican camp and began making their way upstream. In a thick fog, at three A.M. on the morning of October 2, the Americans reached the Mexicans and started firing their rifles in the general direction of the camp.

At one point in the battle, the commanders of the two sides—Castaneda and Colonel John Henry Moore—held a meeting on the field. Nothing was resolved, however, and the two men went back to their own troops. At this point, the Americans fired their cannon at the Mexicans. No one was injured, but this became known as the first shot of the Texas Revolution.

Castaneda called a retreat and left with his men. He had been ordered not to engage a superior force, or to do anything that could embarrass Mexico. The only battle injuries had been a minor gunshot wound and a bloody nose—

Antonio Lopez de Santa Anna

"6th Texas Calvary, Gould's battalion flag."
star and Texas shield Confederate variant

Stephen F. Austin Texas flag design

on the river between San Antonio and the Gulf of Mexico. Whoever controlled Goliad could control the supply lines to the city.

General Martin Perfecto de Cos occupied Goliad on October 1, arriving with four hundred men. Four days later, Cos departed for San Antonio de Bexar, leaving behind less than thirty men to guard the town and keep order.

On October 9, one hundred and twenty Texas volunteers arrived at Goliad and took the Mexican soldiers by surprise. After only half an hour of fighting, the Texans recaptured the town. They had lost no men and only a few were wounded. Three Mexicans had been killed, seven wounded, and twenty-one captured. With the capture of Goliad, the Americans had gained a base of operations at a strategic location.

Late in October, the new Texas Republican Army marched on San Antonio de Bexar. San Antonio was the center of Mexican forces in Texas, the headquarters of the Mexican army led by General Cos. Stephen Austin sent James

caused by a horse that had spooked at the first shots.

After the Battle of Gonzales, the Texans began gathering an army. The Texas Republican Army, led by Stephen Austin, brought together men in defense of the freedoms of the American settlers in Texas.

At the same time as Castaneda and his men sat waiting by the west bank of the Guadalupe River, Mexican troops marched on the settlement of Goliad to the south, on the San Antonio River. Goliad occupied a strategic position, lying

Mission in San Antonio

Bowie and James W. Fannin Jr. with ninety men to look for a protected location nearby from which to attack the town. Cos, realizing the Americans were marching on San Antonio, sent Colonel Domingo de Ugartechea out with 275 men and two cannons to attack the small advance force led by Bowie.

In the early morning fog of October 28, Bowie's men met the large Mexican force in the trees near the San Antonio River, not far from the Concepción Mission. Thirty minutes later, the main body of the Texas Republican Army arrived, but by then the Mexicans were already in full retreat. Only one Texan had been killed, and another wounded, but the Mexicans had suf-

fered much greater casualties—fourteen killed and thirty-nine wounded. Ninety Americans had successfully taken on several hundred trained soldiers.

The Texas army kept San Antonio de Bexar under close watch over the next several months. At one point, they heard a shipment of silver would be arriving from Mexico on a mule train. Early on the morning of November 28, 1835, the lookout, Erastus "Deaf" Smith, saw a train of mules headed toward the town, packs slung across their backs. Excited, he reported back to camp, and Bowie quickly gathered some men to intercept the mules. The fight did not take long; the Mexicans accompanying the mules fled toward San Antonio, abandoning the animals. The Americans followed them a little way, but were more interested in the mules with their packs of silver. They threw open the packs in anticipation, only to discover no silver at all. Every pack had been stuffed full of grass! The Texans did not learn the truth for some time: the night before, the Mexicans had gone out to collect grass for their horses.

Two weeks later, the army of Texas succeeded in their siege and took San Antonio de Bexar on December 9, 1835. After they captured San Antonio, most of the Texas volunteers went

James Bowie

home to their families, leaving only just over a hundred men to occupy the town. The Texans released the Mexican prisoners and sent them south to their homes in Mexico.

Furious at the loss of San Antonio de Bexar, Santa Anna was determined to teach the Texans a lesson. He gathered an army and marched at its head north toward San Antonio. When Sam Houston, now Major General Sam Houston of the Texas Army, heard about Santa Anna's approach, he ordered the men at San Antonio de Bexar to abandon the town, since he had no time to send reinforcements. The Americans ignored the orders and set about fortifying the old abandoned mission, called the Alamo, just across the river from San Antonio de Bexar.

Colonel William Travis commanded the regular army forces at the Alamo, while Jim Bowie commanded the volunteers. In the middle of February, David Crockett arrived with twenty Tennessee Mounted Volunteers. The Mexicans were close behind.

Desperate now, defending the fort with less than two hundred men against thousands, Colonel Travis wrote a plea for help to the people of Texas and to all Americans. The letter ended with these words: "Victory or Death!"

The Mexicans arrived on February 23, 1836,

and occupied the nearly empty town of San Antonio de Bexar. Santa Anna besieged the defenders in the Alamo and kept up a nearly constant barrage of cannon fire, hoping to wear the Texans down. On March 2, thirty-two men, volunteers from Gonzales, arrived and succeeded in slipping past the Mexican lines and into the Alamo. These were the only men to respond to Travis's urgent letter for help.

The Alamo today

*If something or someone is **culpable**, they are guilty of something.*

On March 6, Santa Anna stormed the Alamo. The defenders pushed back two waves of attack, but with the third wave, the Mexicans reached the walls and began climbing up into the fortress. The Texans had run out of ammunition and could only use knives and the butts of their guns to defend themselves.

All the men defending the Alamo died that day, including David Crockett, the twenty-seven-year-old colonel William Travis, and James Bowie, who was killed as he lay in bed weak with illness. Santa Anna had enforced a policy of taking no prisoners. The only survivors of those inside the Alamo were the women and children, a black slave named Joe, and perhaps a couple of men who had escaped before the fighting began. No one knows for sure the exact number of Texans who died, but it was probably just over 180. The Mexicans lost nearly ten men for every Texan killed.

Santa Anna walked into the ruins of the Alamo just after the fighting ended. The dead lay piled everywhere. Indifferently, he glanced around. "Much blood has been shed," he commented, "but the battle is over; it was but a small affair."

The dictator's officers felt differently. "Another such victory will ruin us," one said. General Vicente Filisola wrote later in his memoirs. "In our opinion all that bloodshed of our soldiers as well as of our enemies was useless, having as its only objective an inconsiderate, childish and **culpable** vanity."

As the Alamo lay under siege, the Convention of 1836 was under way several hundred miles to the north, in Washington-on-the-Brazos. Delegates had arrived on March 1 to draft a Declaration of

The interior of the Alamo

The Alamo

Independence for Texas. Because of the events taking place at the Alamo, the convention wanted to finish the document quickly. That night a committee drafted the Texas Declaration of Independence, and the next day the delegates voted to approve it. Forty-eight men signed the document, including Sam Houston.

James Fannin was now commanding the American forces at Goliad. On March 12, Sam Houston wrote to Fannin, ordering him to evacuate. Santa Anna's army was still on the move. For five days, Fannin did nothing. Then, on March 17, Fannin finally began preparations to abandon the fort. He had waited too long, though. Shortly after leaving, on March 20, Fannin and his men were surrounded by Mexican soldiers. For hours, they fought back, but they had no food or water, and they were exhausted. Finally, they surrendered and were taken prisoner. The Texans believed they would soon be set free and allowed to go home.

When Santa Anna heard about the incident, he was furious his men had taken prisoners. He sent orders that the Texans were to be executed at once.

On March 27—Palm Sunday—the Mexicans divided the prisoners into three groups, marched them out into the prairie, and killed them. Nearly 350 men were killed in the Goliad Massacre.

The massacres of the Alamo and Goliad infuriated the Texans. The Texas Army resounded with cries of "Remember the Alamo!" and "Remember Goliad!" The deaths of these hundreds of men only strengthened the resolve of the Texans.

When news of what had happened at the Alamo, and later at Goliad, reached the American settlers in Texas, they started to flee east toward Louisiana, terrified Santa Anna's army would overtake them. The Texas army withdrew as well, pulling back to near the town of Harrisburg (close to where the city of Houston is located today).

Santa Anna and his army followed, reaching Harrisburg and burning it in the middle of April. In their march toward the Texas army, the Mexicans crossed a bridge spanning a *bayou*. To cut off their retreat, or the arrival of Mexican reinforcements, Major General Sam Houston sent Deaf Smith with a handful of men to destroy the bridge.

At 3:30 in the afternoon of April 21, Houston gave the command to advance on the enemy. With the destruction of the bridge, the only di-

N PINES

ES FARM

iment - Hood's brigade,
restored

A **bayou** is an area of slow-moving water, often over-grown with grasses, leading from a river or lake.

Sam Houston by Martin Johnson Heade, circa 1846

Surrender of Santa Anna *by William H. Huddle*

rection either army could take to leave the battlefield was southwest; all other directions were blocked by bayous, marshes, and the San Jacinto River.

The battle itself took less than twenty minutes. The enraged Texans swept down on the Mexican army, who outnumbered them more than two to one. With cries of "Remember the Alamo! Remember Goliad!" the Texans rushed the enemy. Finally, General Don Juan Almonte surrendered to the Americans, ending the battle. Although only nine Texans had been killed, and thirty wounded, Santa Anna's army had lost 630 men, with 208 wounded, and 730 captured.

Santa Anna had disappeared during the battle. The next day, Houston sent out a search party to comb the battlefield looking for him. In the afternoon, they caught a man dressed as a common foot soldier trying to sneak away through the woods. When they marched him into the camp, the Mexican prisoners recognized their leader and shouted, "El Presidente!"

The Battle of San Jacinto ended the Texas Revolution with a definitive victory. Santa Anna

Colonel Travis's Appeal for Aid

On February 24, under siege at the Alamo, twenty-seven-year-old William Travis wrote a plea for help, which he sent to Texas governor Henry Smith. Copies of the letter circulated throughout Texas over the next week, sent out as posters to the settlements of the area.

Fellow Citizens,

I am besieged by a thousand or more of the Mexicans, under Santa Anna. I have sustained a continual bombard-ment and cannonade, for twenty-four hours, and have not lost one man. The enemy have demanded a surrender at discretion, otherwise the garrison is to be put to the sword, if the fort is taken. I have answered the demand with a cannon shot, and our flag still waves proudly from the walls. I shall never surrender nor retreat: then I call on you, in the name of liberty, of patriotism, and of every thing dear to the American character, to come to our aid, with all possible dispatch. The enemy are receiving reinforcements daily, and will, no doubt, increase to three or four thousands, in four or five days. Though this call may be neglected, I am determined to sustain myself as long as possible, and die like a soldier who never forgets what is due to his own honor and that of his country.

VICTORY OR DEATH.

W. Barret Travis
Lieutenant-Colonel Commandant.

signed the Treaty of Velasco on May 14, 1836, giving control of Texas to the settlers and assuring safe passage for himself back to Mexico. Once back in Mexico, his people blamed him for the loss of Texas and ousted him from power. He would take only a few years to regain his authority, though, and begin his rise to power again.

73

Texas flag and seal design by Peter Krag
Background image is a Republic of Texas three dollar note.

Five

THE TEXAS REPUBLIC AND UNITED STATES ANNEXATION

In September of 1836, the new Republic of Texas held its first elections, and Sam Houston became the first President of Texas. Stephen Austin served as Secretary of State, but he died a few months later. The United States and a few European countries recognized the independence of the new country, but Mexico refused. The Treaty of Velasco, signed by Santa Anna, had given Texas land that had never been a part of the original Tejas province, and the Mexicans could not accept this. The greatest dispute was over whether the southern border of Texas ended at the Rio Nueces, or the more southern Rio Grande.

As President, Sam Houston tried hard to govern the new country well. He thought the best thing would be for Texas to become a part of the United States. The other Texans agreed. In 1836, they voted to join the United States, and the next year they sent a proposal for *annexation* to Washington.

Martin Van Buren had just become President of the United States, however, and he refused to even consider the annexation of Texas. He feared the action could bring about war with Mexico, something he did not want to risk. For the time being, annexation was put on hold.

Annexation means the act of making an area a part of something bigger.

Van Buren

Cherokee Indians

The Republic of Texas faced numerous problems. The government had little money, and they had to deal with attacks by Mexican raiders and by Indians. To gain money, they could sell land to settlers, but the Indians already occupied much of that land. Most settlers would have liked to simply evict the Indians and push them west off their land, as the United States was doing with their Indian Removal Act.

Sam Houston, however, liked and respected the Indians. As a boy in eastern Tennessee, he had spent a lot of time with the Cherokee, learning their customs and their language. In 1830,

he had married a Cherokee woman named Tiana Rodgers, his second wife. As President of Texas, he worked hard to negotiate peace treaties with the Texas Indian tribes. He believed the settlers and the Indians could exist together peacefully.

Even before Texas had become an independent nation, Houston had negotiated with the Cherokee to allow them to settle in eastern Texas, as they were being forced west by the United States government. Initially, the other Texans had agreed to let the Cherokee settle among them, but after the Texas Revolution they changed their minds. For years, relations remained tense between the Cherokee and the Texans, with the Cherokee sometimes joining forces with the Mexicans.

The Mexican presidents who led their country after the Texas Revolution believed Mexico still rightfully owned Texas. To stir up trouble, they sent men north in raiding parties to harass settlers and to convince the Indians to attack the Texans as well. In 1838, Mexican commander Vicente Cordova tried to convince the Cherokee living near Nacogdoches to join with him and his troops in fighting the Texans. The Cherokee had not been welcomed in the area, given them by an agreement with Sam Houston several years before, and they were resentful enough to take Cordova up on the offer. Three hundred Cherokee and one hundred Mexicans declared themselves separate from the Texas Republic and not subject to its laws. In response, Major General Thomas Rusk raised a *militia* and marched to subdue the rebellion. After several skirmishes over the fall of 1838 and into the spring of 1839, the Texans finally managed to break up the army of Cherokee and Mexicans.

In December 1838, Mirabeau Lamar replaced Sam Houston as President of Texas. Lamar's feelings toward the Indians were not as friendly as Houston's. The Cherokee alliance with the Mexicans gave Lamar an excuse to declare the Cherokee treasonous and force them out of Texas. After the Battle of the Neches in 1839, the

Treaty between Texas and the Cherokee

*A **militia** is a military force made up of civilians who train to fight in an emergency.*

Calhoun

78

Cherokee left Texas and traveled north to Oklahoma and Indian Territory.

To protect Texas from the Mexican raiders attacking from the south, the Texas Rangers patrolled along the southern borders. The Rangers had been organized in 1823 to protect the American settlers from Indian attacks in the Texas wilderness. (Today, the Texas Rangers are the oldest law-enforcement organization in the United States with a statewide jurisdiction.) During the Texas Revolution, the Rangers fought in defense of the Texans, and later they served as patrols and scouts. After Lamar became President of Texas, the Rangers fought against the Indians and helped to drive the Cherokee out of the country.

Over the next few years, the U.S. Congress started to consider the question of annexing Texas more seriously. One of the issues that had to be resolved before Texas could be made a part of the United States was whether Texas would be admitted to the Union as a slave state or a free state.

One of those in favor of slavery was John C. Calhoun, a southern politician who served, at various times, as Secretary of War, Vice President, South Carolina Senator, South Carolina Representative, and Secretary of State. Most of those in favor of slavery considered it a necessary evil, but Calhoun opposed this viewpoint, referring to it as "a positive good." As a senator in 1837, Calhoun proclaimed, "I hold that in the present state of civilization, where two races of different origin, and distinguished by color, and other physical differences, as well as intellectual, are brought together, the relation now existing in the slaveholding States between the two, is, instead of an evil, a good—a positive good. . . . I hold then, that there never has yet existed a wealthy and civilized society in which one portion of the community did not, in point of fact, live on the labor of the other."

Calhoun attracted many southerners to his way of thinking, since he asserted that slave-owning was something of which to be proud, rather than ashamed. This viewpoint accelerated the widening gulf between the northern free states and the southern slave states.

In 1824, Texas had outlawed the slave trade, although settlers were allowed to bring in their own slaves for years afterward. The Constitution of the Republic of Texas had affirmed the place of slavery in Texas, declaring, "Congress shall pass no laws to prohibit emigrants from bringing their slaves into the republic with them, and holding

Tenure means status.

*To **emancipate** means to free.*

__Abolitionists__ were people who wanted to abolish, or get rid of, slavery.

*To **ratify** means to approve something formally.*

President Tyler

them by the same ***tenure*** by which such slaves were held in the United States; nor shall congress have power to ***emancipate*** slaves; nor shall any slave holder be allowed to emancipate his or her slave or slaves without the consent of congress."

Since Texas already allowed slavery, and since it bordered southern slave states, it seemed almost inevitable Texas would enter the Union as a slave state if it joined the United States. This alone pushed ***abolitionists*** to argue against annexation.

Unlike Sam Houston, who strongly favored annexation, Texas President Mirabeau Lamar believed Texas should remain independent, expanding its borders west to the Pacific Ocean. When he became President, Lamar ignored the question of annexation, focusing instead on issues such as Indian removal.

In the 1840s, westward expansion became an exciting issue in the United States. Settlers had started rolling west on the Oregon Trail, spreading out across the prairies and onto the west coast. Americans believed in the concept of Manifest Destiny, the idea that God meant for the United States to occupy North America from the Atlantic to the Pacific. In this climate, many Americans thought it made sense for the United States to annex Texas.

In April 1844, President John Tyler signed a treaty with President Sam Houston of Texas (who had been reelected) to annex Texas and make it a part of the United States. When Tyler presented the treaty to the Senate in June, however, the Senate refused to ***ratify*** it. Santa Anna had returned to power in Mexico and had threatened the United States with war if they were to annex Texas.

Settlers brought cattle to Texas

Later, in 1844, a rumor surfaced that Great Britain planned to annex Texas itself. Although Britain did not particularly want Texas, it did not want the United States to have it either. According to the rumor, Britain was prepared to annex Texas simply to stop the spread of the United States in North America and to stop the spread of slavery.

The Texans needed annexation. By 1844, after less than a decade as an independent nation, their national debt had reached twelve million dollars. The Texas government had few

ways of making money, and although they managed nearly to equalize spending and earning, the debt continued to slowly grow.

Houston wanted Texas to join the United States; after all, most Texans were already Americans. To attract the interest of the United States, Houston encouraged the rumor, adding that Texas was considering joining Great Britain.

In 1844, James K. Polk ran for President of the United States on a platform of American expansion. He promised to annex Texas, as well as to settle the disputed border with Great Britain in the Oregon Territory. When Polk won the election in November, Congress decided the American people must be in favor of the annexation of Texas. Just days before Tyler left office on February 28, 1845, Congress approved the treaty of annexation, and Tyler signed it into law. On December 29, 1845, Texas officially became the twenty-eighth state in the United States.

As soon as Texas became part of the United States, Santa Anna recalled his representative from Washington and ended all diplomatic relations with the United States. To protect the Texas border from the Mexicans, President Polk sent American forces, led by Zachary Taylor, to patrol the area along the Rio Grande.

Some people believe Polk intentionally tried to start a war by this action, since he sent American forces into an area still claimed by Mexico. Having gained Texas, Polk was already looking further west, his eyes fixed on

Republic of Texas currency

The Republic of Texas is no more.

California. Mexico owned the land directly west of Texas all the way to the Pacific Ocean. The only way to get that land would be to fight a war with Mexico.

By the time the Mexican-American War ended in 1848, the United States would own all of what is now California, Nevada, and Utah, as well as parts of Arizona, Colorado, New Mexico, and Wyoming. The small step of annexing Texas would quickly lead to the gain of nearly a million square miles of land to the United States—384,958 (997,004 sq km) from Texas in 1845 and 530,706 (1,374,529 sq km) from the Mexican Cession in 1848.

When Moses Austin secured permission to bring American settlers into Texas in 1820, little did he realize the far-reaching consequences of his actions. Texas would change the face of America forever.

James Polk

1536 Cabeza de Vaca and his companions reach a Spanish ship on the west coast of Mexico and return to Spain.

January 3, 1823 Stephen Austin convinces the Mexican government to continue allowing American settlers to enter Texas.

November 1528 Alvar Nuñez Cabeza de Vaca and about eighty other men wash up on the Texas shore near present-day Galveston.

1820 Moses Austin secures permission from the Spanish government to bring American settlers into Texas.

1682 The French explorer La Salle travels down the Mississippi and claims Louisiana Territory in the name of France.

1532 Cabeza de Vaca and three other men (the only remaining survivors of their party) set out across the interior of Texas to search for Spanish outposts to the south in Mexico.

September 27, 1821 Mexico wins its independence from Spain, and Texas becomes a Mexican possession.

1833 Antonio Lopez de Santa Anna, a general and Mexican military hero, becomes President of Mexico.

1827 David Crockett is elected as a United States Representative for the State of Tennessee for the first time.

November 4, 1832 South Carolina passes the Ordinance of Nullification

March 4, 1829 Andrew Jackson becomes President of the United States.

1830 President Jackson signs the Indian Removal Act, allowing states to relocate Indian tribes off of their land and into Indian Territory (Oklahoma).

June 26, 1832 The Battle of Velasco marks the first armed conflict between the American settlers in Texan and the Mexican army.

A scene from early Texas

October 2, 1835 The Battle of Gonzales becomes the first battle of the Texas Revolution.

October 9, 1835 The Texans capture the fort at Goliad in the Battle of Goliad.

October 28, 1835 Jim Bowie and ninety Texans defeat 275 Mexicans in half an hour at the Battle of Concepcion.

November 28, 1835 In the Grass Fight, the Texans ambush a mule train they believe is carrying a shipment of silver to San Antonio de Bexar (it isn't).

December 9, 1835 The Texans capture San Antonio de Bexar, ending a month-long siege.

February 23, 1836 Santa Anna arrives in San Antonio and besieges a small group of Texans who have barricaded themselves in the Alamo.

March 2, 1836 The Texas Declaration of Independence is signed by a group of delegates in Washington-on-the-Brazos.

March 6, 1836 The Mexican army storms the Alamo.

February 28, 1845 The U.S. Congress ratifies a treaty of annexation, which will add Texas to the Union.

March 27, 1836 Three hundred and fifty Texans are executed on Santa Anna's command in the Goliad Massacre.

December 29, 1845 Texas officially becomes the twenty-eighth state in the United States.

April 21, 1836 The Battle of San Jacinto ends the Texas Revolution with a decisive victory for the Texans, and Santa Anna is captured.

May 14, 1836 Texas becomes an independent nation with the signing of the Treaty of Velasco.

September, 1836 Sam Houston becomes the first President of Texas.

FURTHER READING

Alpin, Elaine Marie. *Davy Crockett*. Minneapolis, Minn.: Lerner, 2003.

Bealer, Alex W. *Only the Names Remain: The Cherokees and the Trail of Tears*. Boston, Mass.: Little, Brown and Company, 1972.

Behrman, Carol H. *Andrew Jackson*. Minneapolis, Minn.: Lerner, 2003.

Blue, Rose, and Corinne J. Naden. *The Formative Years, 1829–1857*. Austin, Tex.: Steck-Vaughn Company, 1998.

Bredeson, Carmen. *The Battle of the Alamo: The Fight for Texas Territory*. Brookfield, Conn.: Millbrook Press, 1996.

Downey, Fairfax. *Texas and the War with Mexico*. New York: American Heritage Publishing Company, 1961.

Fisher, Leonard Everett. *The Alamo*. New York: Holiday House, 1987.

Fritz, Jean. *Make Way for Sam Houston*. New York: G. P. Putnam's Sons, 1986.

Hoig, Stanley. *Night of the Cruel Moon: Cherokee Removal and the Trail of Tears*. New York: Facts on File, 1996.

Jakes, John. *Susanna of the Alamo, A True Story*. San Diego, Calif.: Gulliver Books, 1986.

Meltzer, Milton. *Andrew Jackson and His America*. New York: Franklin Watts, 1993.

Murphy, Jim. *Inside the Alamo*. New York: Delacorte Press, 2003.

Retan, Walter. *The Story of Davy Crockett, Frontier Hero*. New York: Yearling, 1993.

Richards, Norman. *The Story of the Alamo*. Chicago, Ill.: Children's Press, 1970.

Sullivan, George. *Alamo!* New York: Scholastic, 1997.

Turner, Robyn Montana. *Texas Traditions: The Culture of the Lone Star State*. Boston, Mass.: Little, Brown and Company, 1996.

FOR MORE INFORMATION

Texas Indian Tribes
www.texasindians.com

Texas Revolution
www.tamu.edu/ccbn/dewitt/independcon

General Texas History
www.tsha.utexas.edu/handbook/online
www.lsjunction.com

Texas Republic
www.tamu.edu/ccbn/dewitt/republiccon

Indian Removal and the Trail of Tears
www.rosecity.net/tears

Publisher's note:
The Web sites listed on this page were active at the time of publication. The publisher is not responsible for Web sites that have changed their addresses or discontinued operation since the date of publication. The publisher will review and update the Web sites list upon each reprint.

AMERICANS TAKE A STAND IN TEXAS

INDEX

BIOGRAPHIES

AUTHOR

Sheila Nelson has always been fascinated with history and the lives of historical figures. She enjoys studying history and learning more about the events and people that have shaped our world. Sheila has written several books on history and other subjects. Recently, she completed a master's degree and now lives in Rochester, New York, with her husband and their baby daughter.

SERIES CONSULTANT

Dr. Jack N. Rakove is a professor of history and American studies at Stanford University, where he is director of American studies. The winner of the 1997 Pulitzer Prize in history, Dr. Rakove is the author of *The Unfinished Election of 2000, Constitutional Culture and Democratic Rule,* and *James Madison and the Creation of the American Republic.* He is also the president of the Society for the History of the Early American Republic.

PICTURE CREDITS

Dover: pp. 69, 81, 86–87
Library of Congress: pp. 24–25, 28–29, 31 (left), 32, 32–33, 36–37, 52
Museum of the Gulf Coast: pp. 20–21
Photos.com: pp. 66–67, 88–89
Prints & Photographs Collection, Center for American History, University of Texas:
p. 56
The Smithsonian: pp. 39, 42–43
Texas State Library and Archives Commission: pp. 1, 19, 47, 53, 58, 62, 63, 71, 72, 74–75, 82–83, 84, 96
U.S. Senate: p. 78
Wildside Press: pp. 76 (left), 80

To the best knowledge of the publisher, all other images are in the public domain. If any image has been inadvertently uncredited, please notify Harding House Publishing Service, Vestal, New York 13850, so that rectification can be made for future printings.

PLEASANT - HILL
APRIL 9TH 1864